5355 4548

 **W9-BGP-727**

THE
FOUR FREEDOMS

Freedom of Speech and Expression

by Bryon Cahill

RED CHAIR
·PRESS·

Please visit our website at **www.redchairpress.com**.
Find a free catalog of all our high-quality products for young readers.

For a free activity page for this book, go to
www.redchairpress.com and look for Free Activities.

Freedom of Speech and Expression

Publisher's Cataloging-In-Publication Data
(Prepared by The Donohue Group, Inc.)

Cahill, Bryon.
Freedom of speech and expression / by Bryon Cahill.
p. : ill. (some col.) ; cm. -- (The four freedoms)
Summary: Protected by the Bill of Rights, the freedom of speech and expression is one
of the most cherished rights possessed by citizens of the United States. Learn how this
right protects the media and explore why this right is important to young people today.
Interest age level: 009-012.
ISBN: 978-1-937529-91-8 (lib. binding/hardcover)
ISBN: 978-1-937529-83-3 (pbk.)
ISBN: 978-1-937529-96-3 (eBook)
1. Freedom of speech--Juvenile literature. 2. Freedom of expression--Juvenile
literature. 3. Freedom of speech. 4. Freedom of expression. I. Title.
KF4772 .C34 2013

342.73/0853   2012951567

Edited by: Jessica Cohn
Designed by: Dinardo Design
Photo credits: Cover, p. 5, p. 29: Dreamstime; title page, p 13: CBS; table of contents: Shutterstock; p. 5:
Thomas D. McAvoy/Getty Images; p. 6: Daily Mirror/Newscom; p. 7: Carol M. Highsmith/Library of
Congress; p. 9: John Elswick/AP Photo; p. 11: NBC; p. 14, 15: AP Photo; p. 17: UN Photo/Andrea Brizzi; p.
18: Photobucket; p. 21: Americans for Tax Reform; p. 23: Bettina Stammen; p. 24: Bernard Thomas/AP Photo;
p. 25: Polaris/Newscom; p. 26: Iconica/Getty Images; p. 27: The Agency Collection/Getty Images

This series first published by:

Red Chair Press LLC   PO Box 333   South Egremont, MA 01258-0333

Printed in the United States of America

1   2   3   4   5   18   17   16   15   14

Table of Contents

Introduction

First Freedom 4

Chapter 1

America's First Amendment 8

Chapter 2

Freedoms Around the World 16

Chapter 3

Promoting Freedom of Speech 22

Glossary 28

In FDR's Words 29

Additional Resources 30

Index 32

First Freedom

"In the future days, which we seek to make secure, we look forward to a world founded on four essential freedoms. The first is freedom of speech and expression—everywhere in the world."

—*Franklin Delano Roosevelt*

The president of the United States gives a special speech at the start of each year. Today it is called the State of the Union. With this speech, the U.S. leader shares important beliefs. The president talks about world events and gives ideas for the days to come.

In 1941, the president was Franklin Delano Roosevelt. People called him FDR. On January 6, FDR stood before Congress. The times were hard. Many Americans did not have jobs. Europe was at war. Yet, FDR encouraged the people with his words. He spoke about Four Freedoms and their importance.

- Freedom of speech and expression
- Freedom of worship
- Freedom from want
- Freedom from fear

Franklin Delano Roosevelt, or FDR, was president from 1933 to 1945. He gave the Four Freedoms speech at the start of his third term in office.

Respect for All

FDR said that the Four Freedoms belong to all people. Freedom from want and fear are human rights. The freedoms to speak and worship deserve respect all around the world.

When he spoke, FDR was standing before the U.S. **Congress**. Yet, he was not talking just to people in government. He was speaking to Americans everywhere. He was reaching out to people around the world, too.

Europe was fighting World War II. Most Americans thought the United States should stay out of it. But in his speech, the president presented the war in a new way. He knew our ally Great Britain was in danger. FDR framed the war as a battle for American freedoms and values.

People in Great Britain were in danger. FDR knew the U.S. would need to help.

The Four Freedoms are engraved on one wall of the Franklin Delano Roosevelt Memorial in Washington, D.C. The memorial features four outdoor rooms, one for each term that Roosevelt served as president.

Fight for Freedoms

Germany and Italy were trying to take over the world. Their leaders made laws that hurt many people. They took away many freedoms. With his speech, FDR made a case to join in the fight against them. He believed that America should help the nations fighting for liberty.

7

America's First Amendment

Congress shall make no law respecting an establishment of religion, or prohibiting the free exercise thereof; or abridging the freedom of speech, or of the press; or the right of the people peaceably to assemble, and to petition the Government for a redress of grievances.

—The First Amendment

The first freedom that FDR spoke of was the freedom of speech and expression. The United States promises this freedom in the Bill of Rights. It was one of the first laws of the nation.

The U.S. Constitution is the agreement that lays out the laws of the land. Its main ideas were approved in 1787. But soon after, the states agreed on some changes, or **amendments**. Ten amendments, called the Bill of Rights, were added in 1791. The First Amendment covers speech and expression. It promises that Americans can say what they think.

Tourists line up at the National Archives in Washington, D.C., to see the Bill of Rights and other historic documents.

Fair and True

In the United States, people are allowed to speak out against the government. They can argue with the people who employ them. They do not have to fear being thrown in jail.

But the freedom to speak is not an excuse for bad behavior. There are laws that protect the standing of people and businesses. There are rules to follow when speaking out. People are not allowed to harm others by telling lies.

The freedom of speech is meant to encourage respect for opinions. This freedom inspires **debates**. People can take different sides to help figure out what is right.

Did You Know?

In 1941, President Roosevelt declared December 15 to be Bill of Rights Day. It honors the date in 1791 when the Bill of Rights was added to the U.S. Constitution.

Freedom of the Press

The First Amendment also protects the press. The people of the press can speak freely. Reporters can bring attention to wrongs. They can stop power from going to people who misuse it.

The press is made up of the people who gather facts and report the news. But it also includes the **media** they use. In early times, news appeared in newspapers. Important stories showed up in books. Later on, people also listened to radio and looked to television. Now, the news also shows up on the **Internet**. These ways to deliver news are protected by the First Amendment, too.

Web sites are protected by the freedom of speech.

Protecting the Media

People who read news online often get the chance to write back what they think. Each day, many Americans share thoughts online. And they can agree or disagree with posts they read. The First Amendment also protects this free trade of ideas.

The same law protects books, the oldest form of media. At times, people complain about certain books or even try to ban them. The Harry Potter books have been pulled from schools many times. The books talk about magic. Not everyone approves of magic. But the law says that books cannot be removed just because some people dislike them. It supports the right of people to think for themselves.

Did You Know?

In 1982, a Supreme Court ruling said, in part, "Local school boards may not remove books from school library shelves simply because they dislike the ideas contained in those books."

A strong media plays an important role in society. The media helps keep people informed.

A Free Press in Action

Even U.S. presidents have to answer to the press. Richard Nixon was the 37th president. He had to leave the White House when reports in a newspaper tied him to a break-in.

Bob Woodward and Carl Bernstein were the reporters. They worked for a newspaper called *The Washington Post*. They were able to show that the president lied about the crime.

Richard Nixon quit being U.S. president early in his second term. It was the only time in history that this has happened.

Watergate Scandal

The crime took place in June 1972. That is when five men broke into an office in Washington, D.C. They were spying. The men worked for a group that was trying to get Nixon elected again. Supporters of the person running against Nixon worked in the office.

The **Federal Bureau of Investigation (FBI)** and the U.S. Senate looked into the matter. At first, people did not understand how big the story was. But many officials planned, took part, or knew about the break-in. In the end, 43 people paid for the crime.

At first, Nixon said he had nothing to do with it. But there were tapes of the president talking about the

break-in. The tapes proved that Nixon was lying. On August 9, 1974, he resigned. The building where the spying took place was called the Watergate. The story became known as the Watergate **scandal**.

Nixon left the White House for the last time August 9, 1974.

15

Freedoms Around the World

"Everyone has the right to freedom of opinion and expression; this right includes freedom to hold opinions without interference and to seek, receive and impart information and ideas through any media and regardless of frontiers."
— *Universal Declaration of Human Rights*

Many countries support free speech and are part of a United Nations (U.N.) agreement that says so. The U.N. has 193 nations as members. Their leaders work for peace. They try to make life better on Earth.

In 1948, the U.N. made an important agreement. It is called the **Universal** Declaration of Human Rights. It says that people have certain rights and freedoms. Not all U.N. members stand behind the agreement. But the U.N., as a group, supports rights such as the freedom of speech.

The United Nations (U.N.) is an international group of world leaders. Their main building is in New York City.

Meaning of Freedom

The idea of freedom can seem simple. But that is not always true in practice. The U.N. agreement comes out and says so. It says that the freedom of speech is "subject to certain **restrictions**." People can act freely only as long as they do not harm others.

Freedoms have different meanings in different places. China, for example, has the most people of all nations. Their law says that they enjoy freedom of speech. But the Chinese government controls news and media.

Their government also decides what comes in from around the world. People from many countries share pictures and ideas on YouTube. But this sharing service is not allowed in China. Instead, the government offers a service that it controls.

China has more than a billion television viewers. But they only see what the government allows them to see.

North Korea's constitution says that its people believe in human rights. But the people are taught that the rights of one person have no meaning. They are made to consider the needs of the group. This makes it much easier for the government to step in to "correct" individuals.

Power of Speech

In countries such as North Korea, people are afraid to speak their minds. North Korea has a leader who controls what is said. The people are not allowed to leave. They can be arrested if they speak out against their leader.

Many times, members of the U.N. have spoken out against what happens in North Korea. The right to speech is related to other rights, such as the right to gather. The nations that agree on these points have laws that are similar. The free countries often join together in speaking out. They want other nations to be free, too.

Spreading Freedom

The belief in freedom has been building over time. Long ago, great thinkers wrote about what it means to be human. The belief that people should have freedoms grew from these writings.

In the 1600s, the kings and queens in England and France gave their people a few basic rights. In the 1700s, the U.S. founders took those ideas further. The United States was founded on the belief in freedom for people.

FDR carried those beliefs farther still. The day he stood up for the Four Freedoms, FDR helped the world see their importance. When World War II ended, many more nations stood behind the same beliefs. Today, the idea of liberty is still spreading.

Did You Know?

The African Charter on Human and Peoples' Rights went into effect in 1986. It is based on similar agreements in Europe and the Americas. It recognizes the freedom of information and expression.

Controls on Freedom

Even free nations do not agree on what free speech means. Brazil, for example, is a free country. But it also has special laws about what can be said.

In 2012, a U.S. company got in trouble in Brazil. The company helps people share pictures and stories online. It ran a video about someone who was running for office in Brazil. The video said things meant to hurt that person's chances to win.

The company was asked to take it down. The people in charge did not see any reason to do so. The U.S. government would have let the video run. In the end, a man from the company had to go to jail. The idea of free speech is not the same everywhere.

In the U.S., it is not against the law to run campaign ads that are meant to be negative.

Promoting Freedom of Speech

"Exercise your free speech right by posting a message online. Compose a poem. Display a bumper sticker. Keep a journal. Write a letter to the editor. Speak out at a rally. Express yourself in the ways that work best for you."

—*The Free Speech Week Partners*

The third week in October is Free Speech Week. It is a celebration of the right of expression. The U.S. groups that take part include lawyers, schools, and reporters. Free Speech Week also promotes the freedom of the press.

The people in charge encourage students to join the celebration. The way to celebrate, they say, is to speak up about something that matters. They want everyone to use the freedom to speak.

The Free Speech Week group wants all people to use their freedom by speaking or writing about something.

A teacher holds a copy of *The Lorax* which was banned in some areas because of its negative representation of forestry.

Supporting Free Speech

Article 19 is another group that works for free speech. Their name comes from the U.N. agreement about rights. In that agreement, it is Article 19 that talks about the freedom of speech.

Teaching people about rights is important. But practicing those rights matters, too. For example, one easy way to practice freedom is to read. Each fall there is a Banned Book Week. To take part, people can read books that were removed from libraries at some time. It is a way for people to celebrate the right to do their own thinking.

Liberty for All

Ideas become stronger when people question them. The free exchange of speech and expression makes a nation stronger. By using free speech, people can help others learn to think for themselves.

Two months before his speech about the Four Freedoms, FDR spoke in Ohio. He said, "We have learned that freedom in itself is not enough. Freedom of speech is of no use if a man has nothing to say."

The president was telling people that having a right is not enough to ensure freedom. In order to have and keep free speech, they must speak up. Freedoms that are not used can be lost.

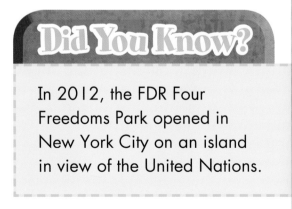

Did You Know?

In 2012, the FDR Four Freedoms Park opened in New York City on an island in view of the United Nations.

Making a Difference

What can you do to help defend the freedom of speech and expression? The answer to this question is simple: express yourself!

Sometimes it can be difficult to talk about things that are important to you. At times it can be tough to find your voice. But if there is something you feel strongly about, there is a reason for those feelings.

Stand Up and Speak

Is something happening at school that you would like to change? What about in your town? Do not be afraid to speak your mind. Just think about your words. When you speak, picture yourself talking in a calm way.

Show respect for others when you speak. But feel confident in your right to add something or say something different. This is your right, too. You can and should share your thoughts with your family and friends.

Use your freedom of speech to take pride in what you believe. Be thankful that you can.

Students find ways to speak up.

The First Amendment gives students the right to express themselves in public schools.

Glossary

amendments	changes or additions
Congress	the law-making body of the U.S. government made up of the Senate and the House of Representatives
debates	discussions, formal or informal, in which different points of view are expressed
Federal Bureau of Investigation (FBI)	an agency of the U.S. Justice Department that safeguards national security
Internet	worldwide system of computer networks
media	means of communication reaching a wide group of people
restrictions	limits or conditions on activity
scandal	conduct that causes offense or disgrace
universal	of or affecting the whole world or all experience

In FDR's Words

In the future days, which we seek to make secure, we look forward to a world founded upon four essential human freedoms. The first is freedom of speech and expression—everywhere in the world. The second is freedom of every person to worship God in his own way—everywhere in the world. The third is freedom from want—which, translated into world terms, means economic understandings which will secure to every nation a healthy peacetime life for its inhabitants—everywhere in the world. The fourth is freedom from fear—which, translated into world terms, means a world-wide reduction of armaments to such a point and in such a thorough fashion that no nation will be in a position to commit an act of physical aggression against any neighbor—anywhere in the world. That is no vision of a distant millennium. It is a definite basis for a kind of world attainable in our own time and generation. That kind of world is the very antithesis of the so-called new order of tyranny which the dictators seek to create with the crash of a bomb.

—from FDR's address to Congress, January 6, 1941

Additional Resources

BOOKS

Caplan, Jeremy, and the Editors of TIME For Kids. *Franklin Delano Roosevelt: A Leader in Troubled Times*. New York, NY: HarperCollins, 2005.

Ditchfield, Christin. *Freedom of Speech*. New York, NY: Scholastic, 2004

Kudlinski, Kathleen. *Franklin Delano Roosevelt: Champion of Freedom*. New York, NY: Aladdin, 2003.

Turner, Juliette. *Our Constitution Rocks*. Grand Rapids, MI: Zonderkidz; Zondervan Publishing, 2012.

WEB SITES

Article 19: *Defending freedom of expression and information*
http://www.article19.org

First Amendment Schools: *Educating for freedom and responsibility*
http://www.firstamendmentschools.org

Freedom House: *Monitoring freedoms around the world*
http://www.freedomhouse.org

INTERACTIVE RESOURCES

Kazaana: *Social media outlet for kids and families*
https://www.kazaana.com

fdr4freedoms Digital Resource: *Videos, biographies, and interactive timeline*
http://fdr4freedoms.org

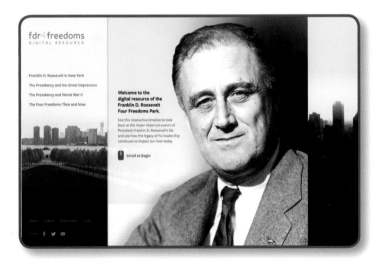

Note to educators and parents: Our editors have carefully reviewed these web sites to ensure they are suitable for children. Web sites change frequently, however, and we cannot guarantee that a site's future contents will continue to meet our high standards of quality and educational value. You may wish to preview these sites and closely supervise children whenever they access the Internet.

Index

Article 19 24

Banned Book Week 24

Bernstein, Carl 14

Bill of Rights 8, 10

Brazil 21

China 18

Congress 4, 6, 8

England 20

FDR Four Freedoms Park 25

Federal Bureau of
  Investigation (FBI) 15

First Amendment 8, 11, 12, 27

France 20

Franklin Delano Roosevelt
  Memorial 7

Free Speech Week 22-23

Germany 7

Great Britain 6

Harry Potter 12

Internet 11, 12, 21

Italy 7

media 11, 12-13, 18

Nixon, Richard 14-15

North Korea 19

press 11, 14-15

Roosevelt, Franklin Delano
  (FDR) 4, 10, 20, 25, 29

The Washington Post 14

U.S. Constitution 8, 10

United Nations (UN) 16-17

Universal Declaration of
  Human Rights 16, 18, 24

Watergate 15

Woodward, Bob 14

World War II 6-7, 20

YouTube 18

Bryon Cahill has been writing for young people for over a decade. As editor of Weekly Reader's *READ* magazine, Bryon wrote short fiction, nonfiction, and reader's theater plays; created award-winning literary websites; and spearheaded an experimental theater adaptation of William Shakespeare's *Much Ado About Nothing* live on Facebook. An avid reader, Bryon also enjoys running and playing tennis at home in Morristown, New Jersey.